Everyday words
used in this book

want
after
here
where
when
who
give
your
know
come

New words
used in this book

how
over
look
love
everything
food
better
use
story
thought

"We will have to let you go."

That is how it began.
I had a job.
Then I did not have a job.

That is how it began.
And this is how it will end.

Here I am,
on the top of a block of flats.
It's high up here
and I can see far away.
I can see where Fran and the kids are.
I can send them my love from here.

It will all be over in a bit.
Don't look down.

It did not help that Fran got ill
at about the time when I lost my job.
I had to do everything.
I did not have time to look for a job.
I had plenty to do looking after Fran
and the kids.

We had no cash,
but I still had to pay the rent.
And we all had to eat!

To start with, I paid for everything
with my credit card.
Then I paid with Fran's credit card.
Then we had no credit left.
Just big bills that I could not pay.

I did not know what to do next.
I had to try to do everything
with no cash.
No cash and no help.

I could not pay the rent.
Some days Fran and I had no food.
Fran could not get better without food!
Getting food was the main thing.
And I could not do it.
I could not feed my kids.

In the end I went to the food bank
to get some food for the kids.
I felt useless.
It's my job to feed the kids
and I could not do it.

"Pay the rent or get out."

That was the next thing.
But what could I pay the rent with?
I could not see a way out.

Here I am then.

Fran and the kids will be better off without me.

If I jump, it will all be over for me and they can start again.

I admit defeat.

This is how it will end.

It will all go away.

I just have to let go...

"Are you all right?
Can I help?
I'm Lea, from the flats.
Do you want a cup of tea?
Come down with me to my flat.
I know I'd love a cup of tea."

"I don't need a cup of tea.
I don't need you.
I need you to go away.
I need to do this.
Fran and the kids will be better off
without me.
I cannot carry on."

"Do you know how much Fran
and the kids love you?
Do you know how much
they would miss you
if you went away?
Who would look after them?
Who would love them as you do?"

"They would be better off without me.
I am no use to them.
I cannot pay the rent.
I cannot pay for food.
I cannot make Fran better.
I am useless."

"I can see you feel bad.

But do you think that they would be
better off without you?

Don't you think they are waiting for you
to come home?

How will Fran pay the rent?

How will the kids get food?

Who would love them as you do?"

"Which do you think Fran would want?
Would she want to have you
and no food?
Or would she want no you
and still no food?"

"There must be a way out.
You just haven't thought of it yet.
This is not the end of your story,
you know.
You have time to add lots of stuff
to your story."

"Just put your leg back over the wall.
That's it.
Give me your hand.
That's it."

"How about that cup of tea?"

Let It Rip

by June Lewis

Set 1: Book 9

Let It Rip
Sound Reads Set 1: Book 9

Written by June Lewis
Illustrations by Stephen Bate
Edited by Catherine White

First published and distributed in 2021 by Gatehouse Media Limited

ISBN: 978-1-84231-219-3

British Library Cataloguing-in-Publication Data:
A catalogue record for this book is available from the British Library

Cover Image: Stock photo. Posed by model.

**Everyday words
used in this book**

you

time

of

have

about

out

there

go

for

my

**New words
used in this book**

angry

anger

died

talk

take

when

your